Presented to:

Martha

From:

Mom

Date:

May 9th 2001

Quiet Moments with God

DEVOTIONAL FOR WOMEN

Honor Books
Tulsa, Oklahoma

Quiet Moments with God Devotional for Women
ISBN 1-56292-884-8
Copyright 2001 © by Honor Books
P.O. Box 55388
Tulsa, Oklahoma 74155

Devotionals drawn from *Quiet Moments with God Devotional* series, including *Breakfast with God, Coffee Break with God, Daybreak with God, In the Garden with God, In the Kitchen with God, Sunset with God, Tea Time with God, Through the Night with God,* and *Christmas with God,* all published by Honor Books.

Introduction

Some say life is *hard* on women. Some say life is *best* for women.

As women we have been called "the weaker sex," "the fairer sex," the "nurturers," the "underpaid workforce," and the "center point" or "rock" of family life. What we lack in physical strength we often make up for in emotional fortitude. Statistically, women make less money than their male counterparts, but women typically live longer—and perhaps happier—lives. We may suffer the pain of childbirth, but we're usually the ones our children run to first with their joys and sorrows. Women are often the ones holding things together in times of trouble—and the catalyst for celebration in good times.

Perhaps it's fair to say that a woman's life is fraught with challenges, but it's also rich in rewards. Where can a woman find the strength and courage, the joy and peace, the love and trust to live her life to the fullest? By making time for God. Quiet moments spent in reflection, prayer, surrender, and thanksgiving can bring refreshment and renewal.

Throughout Scripture, God encourages us to draw near to Him, to come and experience His love and grace, to take shelter in His arms, to seek Him, to know Him, to trust in Him. His loving invitation to enter into His presence knows no boundaries of time or space or schedule or place.

This beautiful new edition of *Quiet Moments with God for Women* will help you find the heavenly focus you need for living. A quiet moment with God is the *best* part of a woman's day.

I AM THE LORD—
I DO NOT CHANGE.

MALACHI 3:6 TLB

The God of Tomorrow

Rebecca was growing weary of the technology: the Internet, cloning, super-computers, spy satellites. Where would it all end?

The world was moving too fast, and she yearned for the sights and sounds of simpler times: the whistle of a teakettle, a real crackling fire (instead of a gas log), the comfort of her grandpa's lap, and the smell of his sweet cherry pipe.

"Grandpa," she remembered asking one time, "did you have spaceships when you were little?"

He chuckled. "No, honey, when I was a little boy, we rode in a horse-drawn wagon to town. Airplanes had just really gotten off the ground."

"But you had trains."

"Yep, I guess I always liked trains the best."

The sound of a train whistle still reminded her of Grandpa and how he looked in his navy-blue conductor's uniform. Sometimes he would let her dress up in it and carry around his big silver watch. "All aboard!" she'd call, and Grandpa would pretend to be a passenger.

What would Grandpa think about life today? she wondered.

"Honey," he'd say, "I've been in some pretty tight places in my day: train wrecks, labor strikes, and world wars. I reckon if God pulled us through all of that, He can see us the rest of the way home."

She "reckoned" He would. The God of her grandpa's era would be the same God in the twenty-first century.

I CAN DO ALL THINGS

THROUGH CHRIST WHO STRENGTHENS ME.

PHILIPPIANS 4:13 NKJV

What's the Problem?

Ever had a difficulty that gives you "2 A.M. wake-up calls?" It could be a project at work, a committee you're chairing, or a crisis in your family. Whatever the issue, it ruins your sleep and saps your energy for the upcoming day.

John Cleese, who developed a popular series of business training films, describes how our problem-solving can take a nose dive into a downward spiral.

> You start thinking, *I'm uncomfortable. I'm anxious. I can't do this. I should never have started to try. I'm not creative. I was never creative in school. I'm a complete failure. I'm going to be fired, and that means my spouse will leave me and*—in other words, you start enjoying a real, good, old-fashioned panic attack.[1]

Problems can seem ten times larger in the middle of the night. But in the daylight, solutions might not be so distant after all.

Inventor Charles Kettering solved problems by dividing them into the smallest possible pieces, then researching the pieces to determine which ones had already been solved. He often found that what looked like a huge problem was already 98 percent solved by people. Then he tackled what was left.

In bite-sized pieces, problems become more manageable. Remember that with God all things are possible. He can give us peace in our darkest nights and bring wisdom with the morning.

I HAVE LEARNED THE SECRET OF BEING CONTENT.

PHILIPPIANS 4:12

Share the Secret

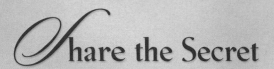

Frances was puzzled by the effervescent happiness of her friend Debbie, who had struggled with life disappointments, including a long-awaited marriage that had quickly ended in divorce and her struggles with being single again. Yet Debbie's whole face smiled anytime she hugged Frances.

"Debbie, how is it that you are always so happy?" Frances asked. "You have so much energy, and you never seem to get down."

With a smile, Debbie said, "I know the secret!"

"What are you talking about?"

Debbie replied, "I'll tell you, but you have to promise to share the 'secret' with others." Frances agreed. "The secret is this: I have learned that there is little I can do in my life that will make me truly happy. I must depend on God to make me happy and meet my needs. When a need arises in my life, I have to trust God to supply according to His riches. I have learned that most of the time I don't need half of what I think I do. He has never let me down."

Frances' first thought was, *That's too simple!* But reflecting on her own life, she discovered how she had thought a bigger house or a better-paying job would make her happy—but they didn't! When did she realize her greatest happiness? Sitting on the floor with her grandchildren, eating pizza and watching a movie—a simple gift from God.

Debbie shared the secret with Frances. Now you know it too.

YOU ARE MY HOPE, O LORD GOD.

PSALM 71:5 NKJV

ight Watch

In 1948 when the Communists invaded Czechoslovakia, President Václav Havel joined a defiant underground that opposed the Soviet government. Twenty years later, when the Soviets seized control of his country, Havel continued to speak out and write defiantly against communism. He was eventually jailed for his activities.

In 1970 several U.S. senators met with Havel in his cell and offered him the opportunity to emigrate to the West.

Havel declined the offer. "What good would that do?" he asked. "Only by staying here and struggling here can we ever hope to change things." Like a watchman in the night, Havel stayed on duty in his country.

Times of trial and struggle often seem like long, dark nights. But doing the right thing—even the hard thing—gives us hope. How do we maintain those long night watches, when there seems to be little change in our circumstances?

- Take one step at a time. Don't attempt to tackle the whole task at once.

- Keep your struggles in perspective. Separate the mountains from the molehills.

- Cultivate the discipline of delayed gratification.

- Learn to recognize the invisible God in the world around you.[2]

Place your hope in the Lord. He will lead you; He will remove your mountains; He will strengthen you, helping you to be patient; and He will open your eyes to His works all around you.

Never Give Up

Because of the seeds you planted, we will one day grow into beautiful plants like this one. We appreciate all you've done for us. Thank you for investing time in our lives.
—Your Students

Grateful tears trickled down her cheeks as the young teacher read the note attached to the fresh green ivy. For months she watered the growing plant and remembered those special teenagers and their gift of love. It encouraged her to continue teaching.

But after a year, the leaves began to turn yellow and drop to the ground—all but one. She started to discard the ivy but decided to keep watering and fertilizing it. Then one day, the teacher noticed a new shoot on the plant. A few days later, another leaf appeared, and then another. Within a few months, the ivy was well on its way to becoming a healthy plant again.

Henry Drummond says, "Do not think that nothing is happening because you do not see yourself grow or hear the whir of the machinery. All great things grow noiselessly."

Few joys exceed the blessings of faithfully investing time and love into the lives of others. Never, never, give up on the seeds you plant!

Let us not become weary in
doing good, for at the proper time
we will reap a harvest if we
do not give up.

Galatians 6:9

Faulty but Familiar

"The Israelites had this cloud, Mom," Ellie's six-year-old exclaimed as the children tumbled into the car after Sunday school. "It was bigger than a thunderhead."

"Yeah, and at night it had fire in it brighter than a streetlight, so no one had to be afraid of the dark," echoed Ellie's four-year-old.

"Every time the cloud moved, the people had to move," the six-year-old continued. "They didn't get stuck in the same campground for forty years!"

As the children chattered on about the Bible story, Ellie thought about the women of Israel and how they must have had to quickly dry the dishes, repack the pots and pans, load everything onto a cart, and follow after God's cloud. Then, when the cloud stopped, everything would have to have been unloaded, unpacked, and reset.

As Ellie walked into her kitchen that day, she thought about the linoleum that was gouged in places and the cupboards in need of another coat of paint. The contents of the overfilled trash can formed a precarious pyramid. The faucet still dripped annoyingly, and the dishes from breakfast sat piled on the counter. Yet with all its faults and peculiarities, it was home.

She sat down quietly at the kitchen table. "Thank You God for my kitchen," she said out loud. "I don't care if it does have drips and gouges and flaws. At least it's a kitchen that stays in one place!"

IN ALL THE TRAVELS OF THE ISRAELITES,
WHENEVER THE CLOUD LIFTED FROM ABOVE THE
TABERNACLE, THEY WOULD SET OUT.

EXODUS 40:36

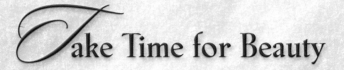

Take Time for Beauty

"He who keeps a little place in his life for beauty," wrote English preacher Leslie Weatherhead, "will find that it does something for him and in him . . . a process that goes on when the beauty is no longer before his eyes and ears, like a seed growing secretly in the dark. God, by a secret ministry, can turn the sight of a snowflake into hope and the sight of the dawn into courage."[3]

Beauty nourishes our souls. Beauty points us to the transcendent, takes us beyond our finiteness, opens our hearts to what is greater than ourselves, and brings us into the awesome presence of the eternal.

A scientist wrote, "If I had my life to live over again, I would have made a rule to read some poetry and listen to some music at least once a week; for perhaps the part of my brain now atrophied would have thus been kept active through use. The loss of these tastes is a loss of happiness, and may possibly be injurious to the intellect, and more probably to the moral character, by enfeebling the emotional part of our nature."[4]

Take time for beauty—stroll through an art gallery, visit a church, linger in a garden, review your mental "snapshots" of a majestic, snow-capped mountain or moonlit night. Allow God to use the beauty He created to awaken in you the desire for more of Him.

One *thing* I have desired of the
Lord, That will I seek ...
To behold the beauty of the Lord.

Psalm 139:14

Living beyond the Thunder

In *The Diary of a Young Girl*, Anne Frank wrote, "I simply can't build up my hopes on a foundation consisting of confusion, misery, and death."[5] She understood that hope originates somewhere beyond our immediate circumstances, that real hope often stands alone in the darkness.

How was Anne capable of courage and faith far beyond her years? She refused to allow the devastation of her times to shape her view of life. In her words, "It's really a wonder that I haven't dropped all my ideals—yet I keep them. I hear the ever-approaching thunder. I can feel the sufferings of millions and yet, if I look up into the heavens, I think that it will all come right."[6]

BE STRONG AND TAKE HEART, ALL

Anne did not survive the Holocaust, yet her words live on. Decades later, thousands have read and been touched by the diary of a young girl facing one of the darkest periods in world history— a girl who chose hope in the midst of hopelessness.

Life sometimes includes hardship. We have the same choice Anne Frank had: hold on to our ideals or drop them. When life circumstances sound like "approaching thunder," remember the simple truth in the life of a young Jewish girl. Holding tightly to one's ideals no matter the circumstance is a hallmark of character.

In all things God works for the good of those who love him, who have been called according to his purpose (Romans 8:28).

YOU WHO HOPE IN THE LORD. PSALM 31:24

A S HE THINKETH IN HIS HEART,

SO *IS* HE.

PROVERBS 23:7 KJV

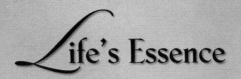

Life's Essence

Ben Patterson writes in *The Grand Essentials:*

> I believe that when life has whittled us down, when joints
> have failed and skin has wrinkled and capillaries have clogged
> and hardened, what is left of us will be what we were all along,
> in our essence.
>
> Exhibit A is a distant uncle. . . . All his life he did nothing
> but find new ways to get rich . . . drooling and babbling
> constantly about the money he had made. . . . When life
> whittled him down to his essence, all there was left was raw
> greed. This is what he had cultivated in a thousand little
> ways over a lifetime.
>
> Exhibit B is my wife's grandmother. . . . She would reach
> out and hold the hands of those sitting beside her, a broad,
> beatific smile would spread across her face, her dim eyes
> would fill with tears as she looked up to heaven and . . .
> poured out her love to Jesus. . . . She loved Jesus and she
> loved people. . . . She couldn't keep her hands from patting
> us lovingly whenever we got near her. When life whittled
> her down to her essence, all there was left was love.[7]

The difference in the "essence" that emerged as life waned for each of
these people is defined by their priorities. Grandma Edna did everything
with love for her family, her God, and His children. The uncle's life was
lived only for himself.

When life has whittled you to your essence, whom will you most
resemble: the uncle or the grandmother?

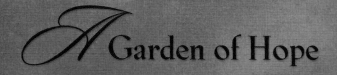Garden of Hope

As Shannon sat by her mother's bedside day by day, she observed the leaves as they changed to autumn splendor outside the bedroom window. And she watched her mother's cancer-riddled body weaken.

One by one, green leaves faded to yellow, then bright orange, covering the ground like a pool of crackling sunshine. The oak tree, now naked and lonely, swayed in the winter breeze. One day Shannon noticed a lone leaf hanging on tenaciously. The same day, her mother's pulse grew weaker, and she slipped into a coma. All that week, Shannon longed to hear her mother's words once again—to feel the springtime of her voice.

Outside the bedroom window, the lone leaf held on. Shannon wondered how it could keep from fluttering to the ground. An inner voice seemed to murmur the answer: *It needs to let go, and so do you.*

The next morning Shannon walked quietly into her mother's room, dreading to see her mother's lifeless form. But her mom suddenly woke up, squeezed her daughter's hand, and said, "I love you, Shannon."

And then, like a leaf that had clung too long, her mother released Shannon's hand—and she was gone.

As Shannon closed the drapes, she realized the leaf had disappeared from the tree. In its place, a new bud was already forming. Shannon knew joy would blossom again. Like the promise of springtime, God would grow a new garden of hope in the fertile soil of Shannon's heart.

SEE, I AM DOING A NEW THING!

NOW IT SPRINGS UP;

DO YOU NOT PERCEIVE IT?

ISAIAH 43:19

Say That Again?

In 1954 Sylvia Wright wrote a column for *The Atlantic* in which she coined the term *mondegreen,* her code word for misheard lyrics. She recounted her own misunderstanding upon hearing the lyrics of the Scottish folk song, "The Bonny Earl of Morray,"

Ye highlands, and ye lowlands,
Oh! Whair hae ye been?
They hae slaine the Earl of Murray,
And layd him on the green.

She misheard the last line as "and Lady Mondegreen." It saddened her immensely that both the Earl and the Lady had died. Of course, she was later chagrined to learn that those were not the lyrics at all.

Since then, mondegreen collectors have been on the lookout for newer and more comical misunderstandings. For example:

In "America the Beautiful," one young patriot heard, "Oh beautiful, for spaceship guys."

Another considered "Away in a Manger" a little unsettling as he sang, "the cattle are blowing the baby away."

Then there was the Mickey Mouse Club fan who, when the cast sang "Forever hold your banners high," thought they were encouraging her to "Forever hold your Pampers high!"

. It's no wonder that, with all our earthly static and clamor, we sometimes think we're singing the right words when we're not. But if we begin each day in quiet conversation with God, His Word comes through loud and clear. There can be no misunderstanding God's lyrics.

SO SHALL MY WORD BE THAT GOES FORTH FROM MY
MOUTH; IT SHALL NOT RETURN TO ME VOID,
BUT IT SHALL ACCOMPLISH WHAT I PLEASE, AND IT SHALL
PROSPER *IN THE THING* FOR WHICH I SENT IT.

ISAIAH 55:11 NKJV

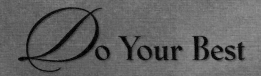

Do Your Best

Martin Luther, the sixteenth-century German theologian who initiated the Protestant Reformation, sounds like a man who would be eminently sure of himself. Anyone who would dare to publicly question the Church—in a time when it could cost him his life—could not be a man who had doubts. Right?

Wrong. Luther spent his early years obsessed with his presumed unworthiness. He periodically fasted and mistreated his body in an attempt to "earn" God's favor. On a pilgrimage to Rome, he climbed the Steps of Pilate on his knees, kissing each step. He constantly confessed his sins to God, yet he never felt he had done enough.

One day while reading the book of Romans, Luther realized he could not earn his salvation. (See Romans 4:13-14.) Luther felt liberated and radically changed his opinions about works and grace. He recognized Jesus Christ had already done all the "earning" necessary for his salvation. He simply needed to *receive* what Jesus had done on the cross.

Even when we fall flat on our faces in failure or just feel low, our mistakes are not the end of the world. Our inadequacy is not our doom. Our salvation doesn't depend on how well we manage to color inside the lines!

Perfection may be our aim, but when we fail, we can pray, "Forgive me, Lord, for what I have done, for what I have left undone. I trust You to be my Savior, my Deliverer, and my Hope." He is, and He always will be.

Whoever calls on the name of the Lord will be delivered.

Joel 2:32 NASB

I WILL BLESS THEM AND THE PLACES

SURROUNDING MY HILL.

I WILL SEND DOWN SHOWERS IN SEASON;

THERE WILL BE SHOWERS OF BLESSING.

EZEKIEL 34:26

Be a Blessing Counter

"Oh no, not again," Wendy moaned as she awoke from a sound sleep. For several nights, she had awakened in the middle of the night, unable to get back to sleep. She tried counting sheep and drinking warm milk, but she remained wide awake, worrying about the cause of her problem. During the day, she found it hard to focus on her work, and the dark rings under her eyes made her look and feel older.

One sleepless night, Wendy picked up her Bible and began to read. After many nights, she began to understand the Bible's message of peace. Her sheep counting changed to blessing counting, and she discovered that she always fell asleep before she could count them all.

Instead of dreading her insomnia, she looked forward to studying the Bible in the middle of the night. God's power and presence filled her soul with strength and self-worth. For the first time, she felt in control and began to believe that she could do all things through Christ.

Eventually Wendy's insomnia faded away, and her sleep grew sweet. But she made sure to spend time alone with God during the day. God had used those sleepless nights to teach her the truth of living and the joy of loving. By counting blessings, she learned that the answer to peaceful sleep is, not in counting sheep, but in calling on the Shepherd.

ight Driving

A woman confessed to a friend her confusion and hesitancy about an important life decision she was facing. She professed belief in God but struggled with faith for choosing her path.

"How can I know I'm doing the right thing?" she asked. "How can I possibly believe my decision will be right when I can't even see tomorrow?"

Her friend counseled her, "When you're driving down a dark country road with no street lights to give you any notion of where you are, it's a little scary. But you rely on headlights. They may only show you ten yards of road in front of you, but you see where to go for that little stretch. And as you travel that ten-yard stretch of road, the headlights show you ten more yards, and ten more, until eventually you reach your destination safe and sound. "That's how I feel about living by faith. I may not be able to see tomorrow, next week, or next year, but I know that God will give me the light to find my way when I need it."

When you come to the edge of all the light you know and are about to step off into the darkness of the unknown, faith is knowing one of two things will happen: There will be something solid to stand on, or you will be taught how to fly.

—Barbara J. Winter

THY WORD IS A LAMP UNTO MY FEET, AND LIGHT UNTO MY PATH.

PSALM 119:105 ASV

CASTING ALL YOUR CARE UPON HIM;

FOR HE CARETH FOR YOU.

1 PETER 5:7 KJV

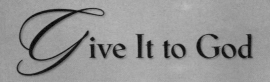

Give It to God

Very often it's not the crises of life that get to us, but the little things that wear us down. We can learn a lesson from the oyster:

There once was an oyster whose story I tell,
Who found that sand had got under his shell;
Just one little grain, but it gave him much pain,
For oysters have feelings although they're so plain.
Now, did he berate the working of Fate,
Which had led him to such a deplorable state?
Did he curse out the government, call for an election?
No; as he lay on the shelf, he said to himself:
"If I cannot remove it, I'll try to improve it."
So the years rolled by as the years always do,
And he came to his ultimate destiny—stew.
And this small grain of sand which had bothered him so,
Was a beautiful pearl, all richly aglow.
Now this tale has a moral—for isn't it grand
What an oyster can do with a morsel of sand?
What couldn't we do if we'd only begin
*With all of the things that get under our skin?*⁹

THE LORD MAKE YOU INCREASE
AND ABOUND IN LOVE ONE TOWARD ANOTHER,
AND TOWARD ALL *MEN*.

1 THESSALONIANS 3:12 KJV

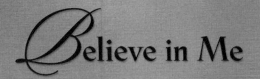elieve in Me

    Cynthia was amazed and grateful for what she was seeing. Ms. Nelson, a fifth-grade teacher at the private school where Cynthia worked, was quietly greeting the children and their parents at the door of her classroom. Ms. Nelson spoke with pride to each parent of the work of his or her child. She took time to mention the child by name and to point out something on that child's work that was particularly noteworthy. As a result, both the parent and the child glowed with satisfaction.

    This was not a special event—it was the morning of a normal school day, and Ms. Nelson made it a habit to be at the door every morning.

    Later that afternoon, Cynthia asked her fifth-grade son, John, how he liked being in Ms. Nelson's class. John responded, "I like it a lot. She is a really neat teacher because you always know that she believes in you. Even when you don't get everything right, she still believes in you."

    What a gift—the ability to believe in others and communicate it to them daily, just as our Lord loves and believes in us without fail. We can all learn to pass this gift on to those we care about.

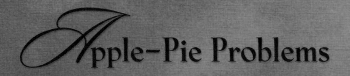

Apple-Pie Problems

Peel. Core. Season. Mix. The steps for making Marilyn's favorite apple pie rolled from her fingertips without a pause. The pie crust lay trimmed and ready in the pie pan, awaiting the seasoned filling. She sprinkled walnuts on top of the filling and placed the top crust into position. A heavy sigh escaped from her lips. It was a good thing that this was a familiar recipe. Marilyn's mind was not on the pie, but rather on a troubled relationship with a close friend. With each day, things only seemed to grow worse. *What do I do now?* she wondered.

As she slid the pie into the oven, Marilyn remembered her prayer journal. She began to write a letter to God, pouring out her heart and her hurt about this troubled relationship. Before she knew it, the oven timer sounded, so she closed the journal and sniffed the familiar warm scent of apples filling the room.

Her heart felt lighter. She was struck by the similarity between the pie and the prayer journal. Wrapped between two pie crusts and left to time and the work of the oven, the apples were still apples, but their taste and texture had changed from tart and crisp to sweet and smooth.

Marilyn had wrapped her concerns between the covers of prayer. As she set the pie on top of the stove, God reassured her that all she needed was to give Him time to work. He would change that soured relationship and make things sweet again.

He who was seated on the throne said, "I am making everything new!"

Revelation 21:5

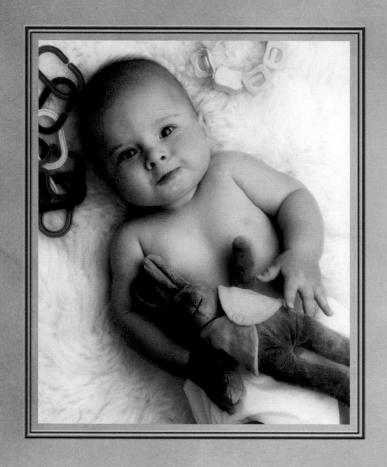

HE HAS MADE EVERYTHING

APPROPRIATE IN ITS TIME.

ECCLESIASTES 3:1L NASB

A Time to Pray

Several years ago a television ad focused on a lovely young woman's smiling face. She was looking down and obviously very busy at the task before her, although what she was doing was not shown. At the same time she was busy with this task, she was praying. The ad's emphasis was on taking time to pray, no matter what else we must do during the day.

As the camera moved away from this young woman's face and down to what she was doing, it became clear that this was a young mother diapering her baby.

What a lovely picture of how easy it is for us to talk with the Lord. During each twenty-four-hour day, we can creatively find a portion of time that is just for God—a time of genuine communication with the Lord.

We mutter and sputter,
We fume and we spurt,
We mumble and grumble,
Our feelings get hurt.
We can't understand things,
Our vision grows dim,
When all that we need is
A moment with Him.

God wants this time with us and we need it with Him. There are times we can be alone with the Savior, but we may have to be creative in looking for those moments. Early, late, long, or short, time spent with God is the most precious of all.

BECAUSE OF THE LORD'S GREAT LOVE

WE ARE NOT CONSUMED,

FOR HIS COMPASSIONS NEVER FAIL.

THEY ARE NEW EVERY MORNING;

GREAT IS YOUR FAITHFULNESS.

LAMENTATIONS 3:22–23

The Spice of Life

Most of us have a routine we follow when we awake, when we get to work, when we're home, and even on weekends. Have you come to dread another sink full of dishes, another load of laundry, another car to wash, another lawn to mow, another rug to vacuum, or another floor to scrub? Is there any end to the "routine" of life?

There's no getting out of most of those chores. Someone has to keep things clean and running smoothly. The one thing we can control is our attitude toward it all.

Rather than emphasizing the "same old," we should remember what the Bible says: *I will give you a new heart and put a new spirit in you* (Ezekiel 36:26). God wants us to embrace life and keep our eyes open for new possibilities, our minds open to new ideas, and our hearts open to new people who cross our path.

Even in the midst of routine, God can bring something new, unusual, and different. Sometimes upsetting the routine can be distressing. But don't let it shake your confidence in God's plan for your life; let it enhance His plan.

Whether life seems to have a "sameness" or has turned chaotic, you are always changing inside. Through it all, the Lord is continually stirring new life within you, giving you new dreams and goals, and molding you to be more like Jesus.

Thank-You Notes

Most of us really appreciate receiving a note saying, "Thanks." It may contain only a few sentences; it may be typed or handwritten. Just knowing that someone took the time to write a word of thanks for something we said or did can leave a warm feeling in our hearts.

The person who sent the note benefits as well. When we take the time to sit down and collect our thoughts and put them onto paper, we are actually taking time to dwell on the nature of the one who has done something for us. We find ourselves grateful for more than just one simple favor or gift.

We say thanks to God when we pray before meals. We often say thanks before we go to bed too. But why not write a thank-you note to God? Do you have a roof over your head? Food to eat? Friends and family who love you? Is the sun shining today? Thank God for those things.

When you finish your note, date it, sign it, and put it away in the back of your Bible. You may forget the note is there, but be assured that you'll find it at an opportune moment, and you'll be reminded to say, "Thank You," again for the great things God has done for you.

SPEAKING THE TRUTH IN LOVE.

EPHESIANS 4:15 KJV

Life Lessons

"You know that what you did was wrong, don't you?"

The words echoed in Sandra's mind as she went home from school that evening. She was a good student who had never cheated in her life. Yet, this assignment overwhelmed her, and in a moment of desperation, she copied the work of another student.

Her teacher, Mrs. Wallace, spoke privately with her, asking if it really was her work.

"Yes," she squeaked out, wondering why she was lying.

Looking her straight in the eye, Mrs. Wallace said, "Take tonight to think about your answer, and I will ask you again in the morning if this is your work."

It was a long night for Sandra. She was a junior in high school with a well-deserved reputation for honesty and kindness. She had never cheated before, and now she had compounded her mistake by deliberately lying—and to someone she admired and loved. The next morning she was at Mrs. Wallace's classroom door long before school to confess her misdeed. She received the appropriate consequences, a zero on the assignment and (her first and only) detention.

Years later, Sandra often thought of that experience and felt gratitude for loving correction from someone she respected. Mrs. Wallace was willing to help Sandra make honest choices—even on the heels of making a dishonest one. For Sandra, this was a life lesson about taking responsibility for past mistakes and choosing honesty, no matter what the consequences.

WAIT ON THE LORD; BE OF GOOD COURAGE, AND HE SHALL STRENGTHEN YOUR HEART.

PSALM 27:14 NKJV

But When?

We have often smiled knowingly at that kitchen-magnet quip, "Lord, give me patience, and give it to me *now!*" And why not? Our society expects immediate accomplishment in almost everything we do—from microwave meals in minutes to global communication in seconds.

It seems, whatever the problem, there should be a button, switch, or pill to deliver fast results. This makes it all the more difficult to accept that, like it or not, spiritual growth takes time.

In a garden, all seedlings have average schedules of development. But as human beings with unique histories and needs, we can't rely on averages to determine when we might take that next step in our walk with God.

It's tempting, when faced with a personality flaw or some growth issue, to pray for and expect immediate change. Sometimes it happens. But how lost and confused we feel if our prayers *don't* bring the instant relief we seek.

During such times, it's good to remember that all facets of our nature—whether traits we love about ourselves or those we want to improve—are part of our God-created being. Even our less-than-desirable parts are there for a reason and contain His lessons for us.

When change seems to come slowly, don't give up hope. Consider that the timetable for your growth is in the Lord's hands. Continue your daily communion with God and trust Him to make you whole *in His time.*

The Greatest Artist Paints Daily

Peter the Great ruled from a palace filled with some of the most exquisite works of art produced in the world. Yet he wondered how men could be so foolish not to rise every morning to behold one of the most glorious sights in the universe: sunrise.

"They delight," he said, "in gazing on a picture, the trifling work of a mortal, and at the same time neglect one painted by the hand of the Deity Himself. For my part, I am for making my life as long as I can, and therefore sleep as little as possible."

He believed that rising early to drink in the beauty of God's marvelous work of art would seem to add days to his life. Psychologists say that getting up early and spending some quiet time enjoying a sunrise can alleviate stress!

Chicago produce dealer John Cooper Smith actually mentioned morning in his will. "To my remaining relatives I give the sunshine, the birds and the bees, wherever the above mentioned sunshine, birds and bees may be found. The greatest art exhibit you will ever see opens daily at dawn. And equally wonderful, this exhibit is always free to those who view it."

How long has it been since you have seen a sunrise? This grand display of God's creativity can ignite the creative gifts He has placed in you and inspire you to use them during the day!

Have you not known? Have you not heard?
The everlasting God, the Lord,
The Creator of the ends of the earth,
Neither faints nor is weary.

Isaiah 40:28 NKJV

What Difference Can You Make?

Annie, who volunteered at a homeless shelter, wondered if her efforts were making any difference to the men who spent most of their days living on the streets. How could carrying coffee or sandwiches to these destitute people make a lasting impact for Christ?

One day Annie ministered to Vincent, who lived in a makeshift shack off a nearby boulevard. Everyone liked him—he was personable and fun and a great talker. But Vincent had a drug addiction that controlled his life, driving him to break into downtown businesses and steal money. Ultimately he was arrested and jailed.

While in prison, Vincent dedicated his life to God and single-handedly won more than eighty prisoners to Christ. On his third day in prison, Vincent died of a massive heart attack. Although Annie didn't personally lead Vincent in his prayer of dedication to God, she was thrilled to share in the fruit of Vincent's harvest. Ministering and carrying sandwiches to Vincent proved to be time well spent.

Annie is just one person to whom God has given a special love for the homeless. Vincent was just one person with a heart of gratitude and a desire to share what God had done for him. Jesus was just one man, and through Him God saved the whole world.

I have planted, Apollos watered;
but God gave the increase.

1 Corinthians 3:6 KJV

"THIS SON OF MINE WAS DEAD

AND IS ALIVE AGAIN;

HE WAS LOST AND IS FOUND."

LUKE 15:24

Come Home

Once there was a widow who lived in a miserable attic with her son. Years before, the woman had married against her parents' wishes and had gone to a foreign land with her husband.

Her husband had proved irresponsible and unfaithful, and after a few years he died without having made any provision for her and their child. It was with the utmost difficulty that she managed to scrape together the bare necessities of life.

The happiest times in the child's life were when the mother took him in her arms and told him about his grandfather's house in the old country. She told him of the grassy lawn, the noble trees, the wild flowers, the lovely paintings, and the delicious meals. The child had never seen his grandfather's home, but he was sure it was the most beautiful place in all the world.

One day the postman knocked at the attic door. The mother recognized the handwriting on the envelope, and with trembling fingers she broke the seal. There was a check and a slip of paper with just two words: "Come home."

Like this father—and the father of the Prodigal Son—our heavenly Father opens His arms to receive us. God welcomes us into His healing presence as children redeemed by the blood of His Son. There, He assures us that He understands our hurts and shortcomings and, miracle of all miracles, loves us anyway.

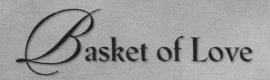

Basket of Love

Every Thursday Jean hustled off to visit the people on her list. Some resided in nursing homes, others were lonely at home. Though she, too, was a senior, Jean was thankful she could still drive. She filled a wicker basket with bananas or flowers and sometimes included a cassette tape of her church's Sunday service. Most of all, she packed her basket with lots of love.

Jean often sat at the bedside of an unresponsive, elderly woman. Although the woman did not seem to know, Jean treated her tenderly as though she heard and understood every word. Jean chatted about current happenings, read Scripture, prayed, then kissed her good-bye at the end of the visit and said, "I'll see you next week."

As Jean's friends began to pass away, she felt sad, but she never stopped serving the Lord. She just found new friends and kept sharing God's love until He called her home.

Like a sturdy basket used for a variety of practical needs, Jean filled her heart and life with love for others. God continues to use His children to help others as long as we are willing to carry around His love. Whether we minister to others through prayer, meeting physical needs, sending cards, or just by a telephone call, we can all serve in some way.

Jean didn't just believe in God, she lived her faith by sharing her basket of God's love with all those around her.

THEY WILL STILL YIELD FRUIT IN OLD AGE;

THEY SHALL BE FULL OF SAP

AND VERY GREEN.

PSALM 92:14 NASB

THE GIFT OF GOD IS ETERNAL LIFE IN CHRIST

JESUS OUR LORD.

ROMANS 6:23

A Package or a Gift?

A gaily wrapped package rested on the kitchen counter as Stephanie and her friends streamed through the back door after school. The girls exclaimed, "Open it, Steph! It must be for you!" Her mother, Leslie, joined the excited girls.

"It's so pretty, I almost hate to open it," Stephanie said. "Maybe I should wait until later."

"No!" her friends cried, urging her to open the package immediately to see what was inside.

Armed with their encouragement, Stephanie grinned and tore off the wrappings. Prying open the small box, she gasped and quickly gave her mother a kiss. "It's just what I wanted!" she cried as she pulled the stuffed animal out of the tissue paper and showed the cuddly canine to her friends.

Stephanie's reaction reminded Leslie of the way she approached God—hesitantly. God offers us the gift of grace, the gift of peace, the gift of talents and abilities, the gift of love, and the gift of eternal life. But all too often we stand and stare at God's packages and comment on how nice they are. We hesitate to accept the gifts as our own.

Unopened, Stephanie's present was just a pretty package. But when she accepted the present as her own and opened it, the package became a true gift from her mother's heart.

Does God have a package waiting for you to open?

A New Look

In 1998, twenty-one-year-old Se Ri Pak became the newest "wonder kid" of women's professional golf, winning the U.S. Open and later becoming the first woman to shoot 61 in an LPGA event. Because she played golf for only six years before turning professional, her amazing ascent was attributed, not only to talent, but also to a fierce mental focus based in the Asian tradition of controlling one's emotions.

Onlookers are awed at the young player's ability to ignore distractions on the course. She won't even walk with nor talk with her caddy because she is intensely focused.

Yet Se Ri broke into tears for the first time in her life upon winning the U.S. Open. Emotional display is unusual for her, but she explains how she's working to change that habit:

> I usually look very serious, but after I started
> playing golf at 14, I saw Nancy Lopez on TV.
> I didn't know she was a great golfer—all I knew
> was that she always smiled. My goal is to be that
> way too. Now when I sign autographs, I always
> put a smile by my name. . . . Even if I don't
> win, I want to give people a smile.[12]

It is said that a smile is the best way to improve your appearance. It's also one of the nicest things you can do for others. Pass it on!

HAPPY ARE THE PEOPLE WHO ARE
IN SUCH A STATE; HAPPY ARE THE PEOPLE
WHOSE GOD IS THE LORD!

PSALM 144:15 NKJV

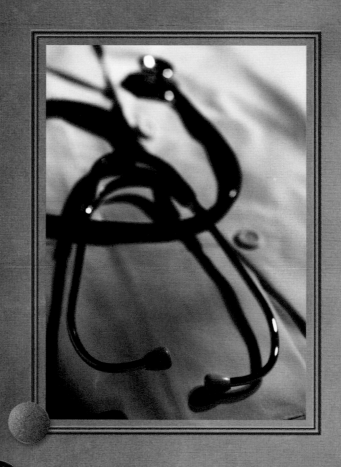

IN THE DAY OF TROUBLE

HE WILL KEEP ME SAFE IN HIS DWELLING;

HE WILL HIDE ME IN THE SHELTER OF HIS TABERNACLE

AND SET ME HIGH UPON A ROCK.

PSALM 27:5

Easy as A, B, C

"We need to run some tests." Those are words you never want to hear from a doctor. Inundated as we are with medical bulletins, our first inclination is to expect the worst. Especially intimidating are the machines used to diagnose our disorders. The Magnetic Resonance Imager (MRI), with its oh-so-narrow magnetic metal tunnel, can bring out the claustrophobia in all of us.

Why not try what one woman did to use the time constructively? Once inside the chamber, she found herself on the verge of panic. Then she remembered some advice her pastor had given her: When things are going badly for you, pray for someone else.

To simplify things, she decided to pray alphabetically. She prayed for Albert's sore knee, Amy's decision about work, and Andrew's upcoming final exams. She moved on to B and continued through the alphabet. By the letter D, she was totally oblivious to her environment.

Thirty minutes later, she was only halfway through the alphabet and the test was finished. The next day as she waited in the doctor's office for the test results, she used the time to complete her prayer alphabet. During her appointment, she learned the test revealed no abnormalities.

When you find yourself facing something unpleasant or even a little scary, turn it over to your Father God and watch Him transform it into a special time together.

Let's Try It Again!

Misty gripped her big brother's hand, and her eyes widened at the incredible scene playing out before her. There, atop the best sledding hill in all of Connecticut, her eighty-year-old grandmother was preparing for the ride of her life.

Poised on the toboggan, she sat as royalty, her long fur coat wrapped around her legs and her fur cap pinned perfectly into place. A small push on the snow with her elegantly gloved hand, and she was off.

Halfway down the hill, the toboggan toppled over, and Misty watched in horror as her grandmother tumbled over three times before sliding into a snowdrift. Running full tilt to the rescue, Misty arrived breathless before a disheveled lump of fur.

Rosy cheeks appeared beneath a lopsided fur cap. Snow was encrusted in the hair surrounding her face, and her bright, mischievous eyes met Misty's fearful gaze. With the confident laugh of one who loves God and knows of His care, Grandmother grabbed hold of Misty's hand. "Again! Let's try it again!"

Whether it's an attempt at sledding for the first time in eighty years, or taking the hand of one you love and risking the exposure of your heart, God offers us the peace that brings comfort in the midst of life's chaos. In fact, it gives Him great pleasure. If we ask, God will give us the confidence to step into life's adventures, knowing that His hand will always be there to catch us.

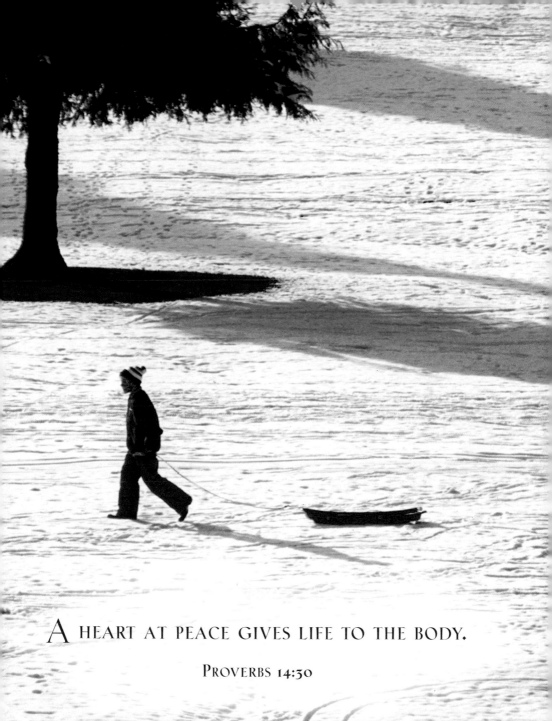

A HEART AT PEACE GIVES LIFE TO THE BODY.

PROVERBS 14:30

torytellers

The Polynesians believe in the importance of teaching the next generation the history of their families. They sit around and "talk story," speaking with excitement and twinkling eyes as they tell the young ones about their ancestry. The listeners sit in rapt attention, soaking up every detail. The children pay special attention so that when they grow up, they will be able to pass the story of their family down to another generation.

Likewise the 1998 blockbuster animated film, *The Prince of Egypt*, tells about the Israelites' escape from slavery and their search for a land of freedom and abundance. Modern Jews tell other similar stories as part of Passover. Traditionally, the youngest child asks why certain foods are eaten and certain traditions are practiced. The answers are told in story form, reflecting on events from thousands of years before and passed on from generation to generation.

Jesus taught by telling stories that even the youngest, most uneducated, and least experienced could understand. More than two thousand years later, those parables are timeless messages about the kingdom of God.

Aesop's fables, fairy tales by the Brothers Grimm, and stories by Hans Christian Andersen are memorable, not only for their messages, but also for their interesting characters and events. Be sure to teach your children the history of their Christian ancestry by sharing with them the miraculous stories in the Bible. Encourage them to pass the story of their "family" down to the next generation.

THOU SHALT TEACH THEM DILIGENTLY
UNTO THY CHILDREN, AND SHALT TALK OF THEM
WHEN THOU SITTEST IN THINE HOUSE, AND
WHEN THOU WALKEST BY THE WAY, AND WHEN
THOU LIEST DOWN, AND WHEN THOU RISEST UP.

DEUTERONOMY 6:7 KJV

WHEN THE HOLY SPIRIT CONTROLS

OUR LIVES HE WILL PRODUCE

THIS KIND OF FRUIT IN US: LOVE, JOY, PEACE,

PATIENCE, KINDNESS, GOODNESS, FAITHFULNESS,

GENTLENESS AND SELF-CONTROL.

GALATIANS 5:22-23 TLB

The "to-Be List"

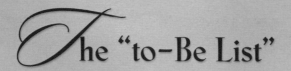

Our "to-do" lists may dominate our schedules, but God asks us to focus on His "to-be" list. It may be important to accomplish certain tasks, engage in certain projects, or have certain encounters during a day, but it is even more important to focus on becoming the person God wants us to be.

Daily we can ask the Lord to help us do the following:
- reflect His love
- display His joy
- manifest His peace
- practice His patience
- express His kindness
- make known His goodness
- reveal His faithfulness
- show His gentleness
- exhibit His self-control

These traits come from a life lived in communication with the Lord. They are the distinguishing marks of His presence in our lives. Our "to-be" list, therefore, must always begin with an invitation to the Holy Spirit to inspire us and motivate us to do good works.

In order to *express* the Lord's kindness, for example, we first must see ourselves as *receiving* His kindness. Then we become much more attuned to opportunities in which we might show His kindness to others. "Being kind" becomes a part of everything we do. The way we do our chores, hold our meetings, run our errands, and engage in our projects are all opportunities to display His kindness to those around us.

When we make our "to-be" list our top priority, the things we have "to do" become much more obvious—and far less burdensome.

Morning Thirst

The need for a refreshing drink when we first awaken in the morning is often so strong that we find ourselves anticipating the taste before we ever get a glass in our hands. That thirst is a driving force that nothing else will satisfy.

There is another thirst that needs to be quenched when we first wake up. It is a thirst we often ignore until it is so great that everything else in our lives—our relationships, our growth as children of God, our joy, our peace—begins to wither.

Patti did not have running water inside her home when she was a child. Not since then has she known that same level of satisfaction a morning drink of water can give. This was especially true if the water in the house ran out during a night when it was too cold or too stormy for anyone to make a trip to the source outside. Sometimes it was a long, long wait for morning.

There is a source of living water that is available to us any time of the day or night. It never runs out, it never gets contaminated, it never freezes over, and it is always as refreshing throughout the day as it was with the first sip in the morning.

Are you anticipating a drink from God's cup of refreshing, living water in the morning? God gives you permission to start sipping right now. Cheers!

My soul thirsts for God,
for the living God.

Psalm 42:2 NASB

IF WE KNOW THAT HE HEARS US—

WHATEVER WE ASK—

WE KNOW THAT WE HAVE WHAT

WE ASKED OF HIM.

1 JOHN 5:15

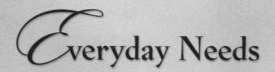

Everyday Needs

"Oh, no! We're going to have to run for the ferry again!" Elaine cried. "And, unless we find a parking place in the next minute or two, we're never going to make it!"

As she and her daughter Cathy struggled through the downtown traffic, Elaine thought about how her daily commutes from home on Bainbridge Island to work in Seattle necessitated leaving a car parked on both sides of the water—and provided plenty of opportunity for parking-place prayers.

"I told you we needed to get away from your office sooner," Cathy chided. "The waterfront is full of summer tourists and conventioneers!"

"God knew about that last-minute customer I had, and He knows we have to make this ferry in order to get home in time to fix dinner and get to the church meeting," Elaine assured her. Then she prayed aloud, "Lord, we'll circle this block one more time. Please have someone back out or we're not going to make it."

"Mom, there it is!" Cathy shouted, as they rounded the last corner. "Who'd think God would be interested in whether or not we could find a parking place?"

"But that's the exciting part of it," Elaine explained. "God is interested in every part of our lives—even schedules and parking places. Now, let's run for it!"

The Lord knows all the circumstances of your day—and your tomorrow. Trust Him to be the "Lord of the details."

The Celebrity Garden

Sherry cleared a spot in her backyard for a rose garden—her dream for many years. As she thumbed through a rose catalog, she sighed at the magnitude of her choices. *Which ones should I pick?* she thought. *A white John F. Kennedy, a large, pink Peggy Lee, a red Mr. Lincoln, the delicate Queen Elizabeth rose?* She decided instead to plant her own "celebrity" garden.

Sherry hurried to her local nursery and bought a dozen roses—all colors and sizes. She worked hard that week, carefully planting each rose bush. When she was done, she decided to throw a party and invite all her friends to help her celebrate her celebrity garden.

Imagine their surprise when Sherry's friends watched her unveil the "celebrity" names she had placed on each rose. One by one, they read their own names beside the flowers. The celebrities in Sherry's garden were none other than her friends. But in the middle of the fragrant bouquet was one called "Rose of Sharon."

"This one is the love of my life, and everything else centers around Him."

A thousand "celebrities" cry out for our time and attention. Relationships, like a healthy garden, need ample doses of love and affirmation. When Christ is at the center of our affection, all other loves will fall into place.

In the garden of your life, who are your celebrities?

I AM A ROSE OF SHARON. . . .
LIKE A LILY AMONG THORNS IS MY DARLING
AMONG THE MAIDENS.

SONG OF SONGS 2:1-2

"Do to others as you
would have them do to you."

Luke 6:31

Kitchen Sink Legacy

Corinna's grandmother never went to seminary, but from her kitchen-sink pulpit she would sermonize while she scrubbed the supper dishes. Her congregation of assembled relatives labored alongside her, clearing the table, drying the dishes, and putting away the pots and pans. Even the children were assigned after-dinner chores.

Corinna wanted to be like the neighbor children who gulped down their meals and left their dishes on the table as they flew out the back door to play. But Grandma would have none of that: "If you don't work, you don't eat." By the time Grandma finished her sermonizing, it would be dark outside, and Corinna would have to wait until the next day to play with her friends. But she quickly learned to do her chores cheerfully, otherwise Grandma would remind her to "do everything without grumbling or complaining."

It seemed Grandma had a saying for every situation. If Corinna was upset about the way someone else treated her, Grandma answered with, "Do to others as you would have them do to you." Or if she overheard one of the kids planning any type of misbehavior, Grandma quickly countered with, "Be sure your sin will find you out." Only much later did Corinna discover that Grandma's gems of wisdom came from God's Word.

Grandma's example demonstrates that everyday chores can be used as an opportunity to share God's love. Why not start a kitchen-sink legacy of your own and let your words—God's words—light the pathway for others?

More Than Atoms

Two young brothers were engaged in their ongoing battle for sibling superiority. Adam, age nine, was explaining to four-year-old Rob the science of living matter, taking no small pleasure in his advantage of a third-grade education.

Soon a skirmish broke loose with cries of *"Am not!"* and *"Are too!!"* ringing through the house. Rob ran crying to find his mother.

"M-o-o-o-m . . . is everything made of atoms?"

"Yes, that's true."

"But, he said I'm made of atoms!"

"Sweetie, he's right. Everything in the world is made of atoms."

Rob sank to the floor, sobbing as if his heart had broken. His perplexed mom picked him up and hugged him. "What on earth is the matter?"

"It's not fair!" he howled. "I don't want to be made of Adams—I want to be made of Robs!!"

We all want recognition for our "specialness." But we should never derive our self-worth from our society, feedback from others, or our own comparisons to others. Our self-esteem should be based in the fact that God created us with the utmost care and has called His creation good.[14]

To Him, then, we are all made of "the right stuff"—and are much, much more than just a collection of atoms!

LET EACH ONE EXAMINE HIS OWN

WORK, AND THEN HE WILL

HAVE REJOICING IN HIMSELF ALONE,

AND NOT IN ANOTHER.

GALATIANS 6:4 NKJV

Everyday Benefits

Blessings we take for granted are often forgotten. Yet every day God "loads us with benefits." Think of some common things you may have taken for granted—and thank God for them.

- Lungs that work steadily.
- Bones that protect vital organs.
- Muscles that hold the bones in place.
- A disease-fighting immune system.
- A heart that pumps blood through a 60,000-mile network of vessels.
- Five senses—eyes to see the dawn, ears to hear a loved one's voice, a nose to smell flowers, the sense of touch to enjoy a hug, and the sense of taste to savor good food.
- Nerve cells that send messages to other parts of the body.
- A digestive system that distributes nourishment.
- The ability—and desire—to get up and out of bed in the morning.
- A place to live and a place to work.
- Loving and supportive family and friends.
- An intimate relationship with God through Jesus Christ.
- The changing seasons of our world and our lives.
- Each day's unique beauty—the angle of the sun, white clouds stretched across the blue afternoon sky, the gold and pink sunset.
- Times for quiet reflection and grateful remembrances.
- The gift of laughter.

Add your own blessings to this list and keep it growing all day long![15]

Blessed *be* the Lord,

Who daily loads us *with benefits.*

Psalm 68:19 NKJV

81

BE STILL, AND KNOW THAT I AM GOD.

PSALM 46:10 KJV

Snuggles with God

A woman who grew up on a Pennsylvania farm fondly remembers her father. Because the growing and harvest seasons were pretty much over from November through March, she grew up thinking that her father set aside that time each year just to be with her.

"During the winter months," she says, "Dad didn't have to work as hard and long as he did the rest of the year. . . . During those long winter months, he had a habit of sitting by the fire. He never refused my bid to climb up onto his lap, and he rewarded my effort by holding me close for hours at a time. Often, he would read to me or invite me to read a story to him. Sometimes I would fall asleep as we talked. . . . Other times, we didn't talk at all. We just gazed at the fire and enjoyed the warmth of our closeness. Oh, how I treasured those intimate moments. As I grew, I thought it odd that other kids dreaded the 'indoor' days of winter. For me they meant the incredible pleasure of having my father very nearly all to myself."[16]

We sometimes experience "winter" in our spiritual lives. The world may seem like a cold place. If you are going through a dry, wintry time, why not snuggle close to the Heavenly Father and listen to His gentle voice? The love and comfort He wants to give you will surely warm your heart.

Touching Life

The sounds of the delivery room receded to a quiet murmur of post-delivery activities and whispered comments between the parents. The father, gowned, with a hair net and masked face, leaned forward to embrace the child as she lay in her mother's arms. The baby was scowling, her eyes tightly shut. With a sense of awe, the mother stretched forth one finger to gently smooth the child's wrinkled forehead. The need to touch her daughter was urgent, yet she was careful.

Developmental psychologists who have examined the process of childbirth and have witnessed thousands of deliveries say that the need to gently touch one's newborn is a nearly-universal impulse, crossing all cultural boundaries. We have been created with an innate need to physically connect with our offspring.

In this sense we are very much like God.

In *The Creation of Adam,* one of Michaelangelo's frescoes decorating the ceiling of the Sistine Chapel, he portrays the hand of Adam outstretched with a finger pointed. Opposite to it you see the hand of God reaching toward man. The two fingertips are nearly touching. No image more clearly reveals the Father's heart. He is ever-reaching out His hand to touch, with gentleness and love, those who are created in His own image.

Mothers and God share a common bond then, do they not? Both possess a deep reverence for the lives that they have brought into the world. Both yearn to touch those made in their image.

PRESERVE MY LIFE ACCORDING

TO YOUR LOVE.

PSALM 119:88

THY NAME, O LORD,

IS EVERLASTING,

THY REMEMBRANCE, O LORD,

THROUGHOUT ALL GENERATIONS.

PSALM 135:13 NASB

Yule Log

It took place around the second week of December every year. Mother would open her cedar chest and gingerly begin to sort through her most prized material possessions. She took such care as she reached inside and one by one removed items that held great meaning to her. Bubble lights, treasured Christmas-tree ornaments, tinsel, and many things shiny and fragrant renewed the season year after year.

One special item was placed on the mantel, transforming the home. It was a Yule log, covered with artificial hyssop and man-made holly berries. A bright red, satin ribbon was attached, and it had a place in the center for a candle.

Each year the family had a tradition of discussing the Yule log and remembering all it symbolized. The log signified a celebration: the birth of Christ. Hyssop, a fragrant herb, was used in ancient Hebrew sacrifices. The lovely, red, satin ribbon signified the blood of Christ that was shed for our sins. The holly berries represented growth, a bountiful supply. And the candle glowed as a loving reminder that Christ is the Light of the World.

Sometimes in the ordinary, sometimes in our traditions, sometimes in our celebrations, we can find the foundations of our faith. Here, a plain log, a few faded green leaves, some old berries, and a tattered ribbon tell the ageless story of God's infinite love.

Kitchen Sabotage

Kathleen's kitchen cupboards and drawers were a mess. The cupboards overflowed with mismatched dishes, receipts, expired prescriptions, and nearly empty bottles of cough medicine. Plastic storage dishes and lids seemed to be multiplying in the bottom drawer. Trying to find a wooden spoon in the drawer next to the stove was like going on a treasure hunt. And odds and ends of twist ties, clothespins, and rubber bands cluttered the silverware drawer. There was no doubt about it. Her kitchen had been sabotaged by the excesses of daily life!

Armed with cleaning supplies, trash bags, and new shelf paper, Kathleen surveyed the kitchen and mapped out her strategy. She unloaded the contents of the cupboards and drawers. Time flew by, and she barely stopped to eat. Soon the interiors of those cupboards smelled fresh and clean, and the only items allowed back were things that were supposed to be there. Then she tackled the drawers.

When Kathleen tumbled into bed well past midnight, the cupboards were done. The drawers were organized. The counters were clear. Her body ached, but it felt good. She had taken a disorganized mess and made it into a useful kitchen once again.

Is there an area of your home or life that has been sabotaged by the excesses of life? Look for ways to set those things in order, then savor the sense of accomplishment that follows.

GOD IS NOT A GOD

OF DISORDER BUT OF PEACE.

1 CORINTHIANS 14:33

SHOW PROPER RESPECT TO EVERYONE.

1 PETER 2:17

Without Words

As with many memorials, the Franklin Delano Roosevelt memorial in Washington, D.C., came into being after years of debate. Women's groups demanded that Eleanor be given appropriate recognition. Activists for the disabled ardently believed that FDR should be portrayed in his wheelchair. On and on, the debates raged. Finally, in spite of all the controversy, it was completed.

The memorial gives testimony to the fact that President and Mrs. Roosevelt served America during some of its darkest years. It is a fitting design, for as visitors approach it, nothing really stands out. All one sees is a flat granite wall, perhaps twenty feet in height, with a simple quote from FDR. But after rounding the wall, visitors move from area to area, each one marked by unique stillness. Visitors see human-sized sculptures of men and women standing in breadlines, read quotes decrying the savagery of war, stare eye-to-eye with Eleanor Roosevelt, and eventually look up to FDR in his wheelchair with his Scottish terrier beside him.

The strength of the memorial comes from its ability to draw the visitor into the presence of one man's passionate belief in serving his country. The impact of the memorial is to make each visitor more aware of the awesome responsibility of leadership—not just the leadership of presidents but leadership of all people.

Whenever you have doubts about your purpose, remember the words of Martin Luther King Jr. as he said, "Everyone can be great because everyone can serve."

Cradled

Two women were eating lunch while riding a ferry across the English Channel from England to France. About halfway through their five-hour journey, the ferry hit one of the roughest seas of the year. The ferry tossed about violently on the waves, to the point that even the seasoned crew felt ill. One woman lamented, "It's hard to eat while you're riding on the back of a bucking bronco!"

When it became apparent that the pitching of the boat was not going to abate, one woman returned to her assigned seat in the middle of the ferry. She soon fell sound asleep and experienced no more seasickness. Toward the end of the trip, after the ferry had moved into calmer waters off the coast of France, the second woman joined her friend. "I was nauseated for two hours!" she exclaimed.

"I'm sorry to hear that," said the first woman, almost ashamed to admit that she hadn't suffered as her friend had.

"Weren't you sick?" the second woman asked in amazement.

"No," her friend admitted. "I simply imagined myself being rocked in the arms of God, and I fell asleep."

All around you today, life may be unsettling and stormy, your entire life bouncing about on rough waters. But when you return to the "center" of your life, the Lord, He will set you in safety. Let Him rock you gently to sleep, and trust Him to bring you through the rough waters.

NOW WILL I ARISE, SAITH THE LORD;

I WILL SET *HIM* IN SAFETY

FROM HIM THAT PUFFETH AT HIM.

PSALM 12:5 KJV

Fine China

Antique hunting one day, a collector found a lovely teacup and saucer. She picked up the cup and examined it carefully. Discovering a small imperfection on the bottom, she lovingly held it in her hands as she thought about what might have caused the cup's flaw.

A few years earlier while visiting a pottery shop, she had watched as the potter chose a lump of clay to work and began to punch and slam it again and again until it was just right. He shaped it, painted it, and fired it into a beautiful piece of earthenware that would be beautiful as well as useful.

The woman thought of her own life with all its flaws, yet Jesus was willing to sacrifice Himself so that she could have a good life with Him. Many lumpy places in her heart began yielding to Jesus Christ, the Master Craftsman, as He shaped and molded, lovingly concentrating on even the finest details. This human vessel was then made fit for His service as He gently filled it to overflowing with the refining work of the Holy Spirit.

As she stepped up to the counter to purchase the cup and saucer, she whispered a prayer, "Lord, help me to never forget what You saved me from, the price You paid, and the hope I have of one day being in Heaven's display as a fine piece, worthy of You."

BEHOLD, LIKE THE CLAY
IN THE POTTER'S HAND, SO ARE YOU IN
MY HAND, O HOUSE OF ISRAEL.

JEREMIAH 18:6 NASB

Volcano Stew

Candy was running late, and by the time she had climbed into her car in the parking lot, the streets were already clogged with rush-hour traffic. She finally stumbled into the house, muttering apologies, and grabbed the pot of leftover stew from the refrigerator. Slamming it onto the stove, she flipped on the burner and rushed to change clothes while hollering, "Someone please set the table!"

A few minutes later, her nose sensed disaster. The stove! The pot of stew that she had placed on the burner was a bubbling volcano. Tall columns of tomato-red sauce spurted into the air above the pot. Pieces of vegetables spewed over its sides. Apparently, in her haste to start supper, she had turned the burner to its highest setting, and now the stew was erupting all over the stove top.

Candy shrieked, and her family hurried into the kitchen. The pot was boiling so furiously that it was impossible to turn the burner off without being spattered by the tomato-sauce columns. The foaming vegetables were spilling over so quickly that easing the pot from its heat source was no small feat. Stew was splattered everywhere, and everyone's hands were covered with the sticky red goo.

Her oldest child broke the silence. With a glint in her eye, she licked the stew from her hands and said, "Good dinner, Mom."

The laughter that accompanied the cleanup echoed the Bible's admonition to always rejoice. If we have God's perspective on life, we can rejoice in everything—even volcano stew.

REJOICE IN THE LORD ALWAYS.
I WILL SAY IT AGAIN: REJOICE!

PHILIPPIANS 4:4

The Lord Directs My Steps

The birthday party was going well, and the thirteen-year-old girl was thrilled that all of her friends could be there to celebrate with her. Each present was "just what she wanted." The last game to play was "Pin the Tail on the Donkey," and everyone was especially excited because the winner would receive a ten-dollar gift certificate for pizza. When the birthday girl had her turn, she lost her footing and stumbled on top of several of her friends.

It was very funny, but the girl wasn't able to get her position right after that, and she continued to try to pin the tail everywhere except near the game's paper donkey. When the scarf was removed from her eyes and she saw how far she was from where she needed to be, she said, "I certainly needed someone to direct my steps."

God has promised to direct our steps. The plan for our lives was laid out before the beginning of time. We can go to the Lord and have a fresh look at His direction.

Are you faced with a major decision? Do you need direction and guidance? Throughout Scripture there are promises that God will show us the right path. We do not have to stumble or grope around blindfolded. Our Heavenly Father is eager to give us wisdom. All we need to do is ask, and He will direct every step we take.

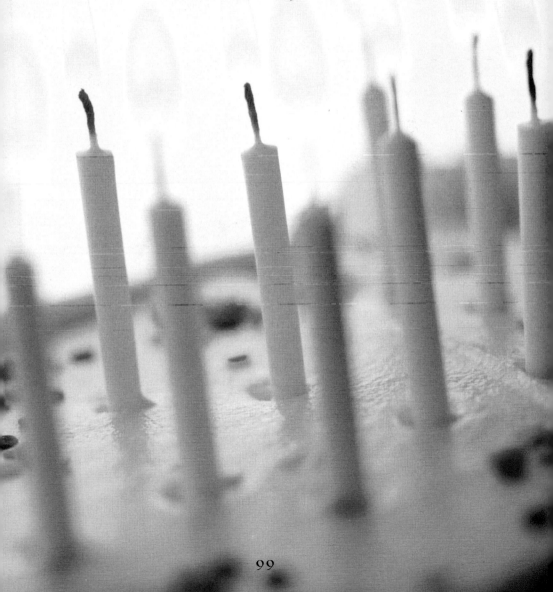

THE MIND OF MAN PLANS HIS WAY,
BUT THE LORD DIRECTS HIS STEPS.

PROVERBS 16:9 NASB

PROCLAIM YOUR LOVE
IN THE MORNING AND YOUR
FAITHFULNESS AT NIGHT.

PSALM 92:2

Love and Faithfulness

How does God love you? Certainly the Lord loves you unconditionally, gently, individually, intimately, eternally, closely, warmly, tenderly, and kindly. You are His child. He always has your good in mind. The apostle Paul said of God's love:

Who shall separate us from the love of Christ? . . .
For I am persuaded that neither death nor life,
nor angels nor principalities nor powers, nor things
present nor things to come, nor height nor depth,
nor any other created thing, shall be able to separate us
from the love of God which is in Christ Jesus our Lord.
Romans 8:35,38-39 NKJV

Proclaiming the Lord's love for you in the morning will give you strength. Because you have a loving Father with you always, you can make it through anything, regardless of the surprises—good and bad—that come your way. By evening you will discover His faithfulness. He sustains you, energizes you, and protects you. All day He provides what you need, delivers you from evil, and leads you into blessings.

His love and faithfulness are precious gifts He offers to us—without end, without measure, without restraint. What joy! Proclaim His love and faithfulness!

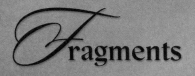

Fragments

Margaret Brownley tells of her son's first letters from camp:

I received the first letter from him three days after he left for camp. I quickly tore open the envelope and stared at the childish scrawl, which read: "Camp is fun, but the food is yucky!"

The next letter offered little more: "Jerry wet the bed."

. . . The third and final letter had this interesting piece of news: "The nurse said it's not broken."

Fragments. Bits of information that barely skim the surface. . . . It made me think of my own sparse messages to God.

"Dear Lord," I plead when a son is late coming home, "keep him safe."

Or, "Give me strength," I pray when faced with a difficult neighbor or the challenge of a checkbook run amuck.

"Let me have wisdom," is another favorite prayer of mine, usually murmured in haste while waiting my turn at a parent/teacher conference or dealing with a difficult employee.

"Thank You, God," I say before each meal or when my brood is tucked in safely for the night.

Fragments. Bits and pieces. Are my messages to God as unsatisfactory to Him as my son's letters were to me? With a guilty start, I realized that it had been a long time since I'd had a meaningful chat with the Lord.

ONE DAY JESUS WAS PRAYING IN A CERTAIN PLACE.

WHEN HE FINISHED,

ONE OF HIS DISCIPLES SAID TO HIM,

"LORD, TEACH US TO PRAY."

LUKE 11:1

"OTHER *SEEDS* FELL INTO THE GOOD SOIL

AND AS THEY GREW UP AND INCREASED,

THEY YIELDED A CROP AND PRODUCED THIRTY,

SIXTY, AND A HUNDREDFOLD."

MARK 4:8 NASB

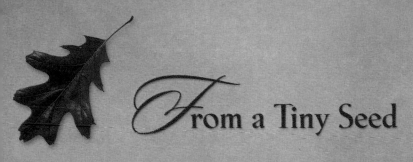

From a Tiny Seed

A century ago a German princess lay dying. While on her deathbed, she requested that her grave be covered with a large granite slab and that stone blocks be placed all around the slabs to seal the grave. She also gave orders for the granite and stones to be held together with large fasteners made of iron. At her request, the inscription in the top of the stone read, "The burial place, purchased to all eternity, must never be opened."

Apparently during the burial, a tiny acorn found its way into the grave. Sometime later, a small shoot began to push its way up through a thin crack in the granite slab. The acorn was able to absorb just enough nourishment to grow. After years of growth, the mighty oak tree broke through the aging iron clamps. The iron was no match for the oak, and the clamps burst, exposing the grave that was never to be opened. New life sprang forth from a deathbed and one tiny seedling.

Every day we are given opportunities for fresh new starts. New beginnings often come when something else has ended. When we allow sin to die in our hearts, we find new life in Christ. Perhaps it is no accident that the mighty oak, which is one of the tallest and strongest trees in the world, starts from a tiny little seed.

IT IS A GOOD THING TO GIVE THANKS
UNTO THE LORD,
AND TO SING PRAISES UNTO THY NAME.

PSALM 92:1 KJV

Sunbeam Blessings

As Gloria sat alone at the dining table, a single sunbeam shone through the closed blinds. What began as a tiny speck at the window burst into a rainbow of color as it spread across the room. It highlighted the old shadow box filled with sentimental treasures.

In the box stood a golden tree figurine covered with her birthstones. She thought of how her mother had celebrated Gloria's birth. Next to it, the animal figurines reminded her of her childhood pets, and the angel watching over a boy and a girl reminded her of playing in the creek with her brother. The baby figurine took her back to the days when her children were small. The fellow pointing to a carving in a tree that said, "I Love You," made her smile. It had been an anniversary gift from her husband. Many fond memories came alive as Gloria spied the tiny angel holding the Bible, and she thanked God for the many blessings in her life.

Even in the midst of difficult circumstances, try to remember the good things God has done for you, no matter how small or insignificant. It will get your eyes off your problems and onto the Solver of problems.

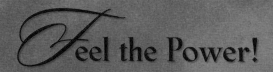

Feel the Power!

Pope John XXIII was once quoted as saying, "It often happens that I wake at night and begin to think about a serious problem and decide I must tell the Pope about it. Then I wake up completely and remember that I *am* the Pope."

How often we imagine that the solution to our problems, the cure for our ailments, or the guarantee for our happiness lies with someone or something outside ourselves. But do we really have so little power?

Martha Washington thought otherwise: "I have learned from experience that the greater part of our happiness or misery depends on our dispositions and not on our circumstances. We carry the seeds with us in our minds wherever we go."

Just think about it. How dramatically would your life be changed if you knew you had the seeds to your happiness waiting inside, longing to blossom whenever you would allow it? From Mother Teresa, in her book, *A Gift to God,* we can learn how to let those seeds spring to life:

We all long for heaven where God is but we have it in our power to be in heaven with Him right now—to be happy with Him at this very moment. But being happy with Him now means:

–loving as He loves,
–helping as He helps,
–giving as He gives,
–serving as He serves,
–rescuing as He rescues,
–being with Him for all the twenty-four hours.

THE FRUIT OF THE SPIRIT IS
LOVE, JOY, PEACE, PATIENCE, KINDNESS,
GOODNESS, FAITHFULNESS,
GALATIANS 5:22 NASB

HOPE DEFERRED MAKES THE HEART SICK,

BUT A LONGING

FULFILLED IS A TREE OF LIFE.

PROVERBS 13:12

Out of the Dumps

We make it through December just fine, no matter what the weather may be, because we are excitedly preparing for the Christmas and New Year's holidays. But then come January and February with snow, ice, subzero temperatures, and the post-holiday blues. Cabin fever sets in, the Christmas bills flood the mailbox, tempers tend to fray, and each day seems like a carbon copy of the day before.

Janet Leighton was suffering from winter doldrums when she decided to take a walk in search of signs of hope. She found them. Red berries, purple briars, and golden grasses would seem insignificant in the spring, but in February they are the promise of more brilliant colors to come. They were enough of an encouragement to send Janet to her Bible, where she sought out well-loved verses and renewed her commitment to God.

The message of renewal seemed to snowball. She learned that a friend for whom she had been praying was being healed gradually, but surely. While paying bills, she saw other ways the Lord had blessed her family, and her spirit was lifted.

Before the doldrums get you down, regardless of the season, take time to look for the splashes of color and signs of renewal God continually sends into your life. They're there. You just have to look for them!

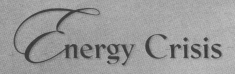

Energy Crisis

Most of us have a series of repetitious chores, errands, and tasks that demand our time and are required to maintain life at its most basic level. "Routine," says Jewish theologian Abraham Heschel, "makes us resistant to wonder." When we let our sense of wonder and awe drain away, we lose the sense of our preciousness to God.

The "daily grind" can cause us to lose our sense of God's purpose and presence. Jesus recognized our preoccupation with these duties in His Sermon on the Mount. He said, *Do not worry about your life, what you will eat or drink; or about your body, what you will wear. Is not life more important than food, and the body more important than clothes?* (Matthew 6:25).

Juliana of Norwich, the fourteenth-century English philosopher, wrote, "Joy is to see God in everything." The psalmist wrote, *The heavens declare the glory of God* (Psalm 19:1 KJV), and the prophet Isaiah declares, *The whole earth is full of his glory* (Isaiah 6:3 KJV). The glory of creation is that it points us to the greater glory of the Creator.

If life's routines are sapping your energy and wearing down your enthusiasm and joy, take time to seek out His love, majesty, and goodness revealed in creation. Be renewed in your joy of who God is—and who you are to Him—and find His strength and purpose in even your most routine tasks.

THE JOY OF THE LORD IS

YOUR STRENGTH.

NEHEMIAH 8:10 KJV

CAST YOUR BURDEN
ON THE LORD
[RELEASING THE WEIGHT OF IT]
AND HE WILL SUSTAIN YOU.

PSALM 55:22 AMP

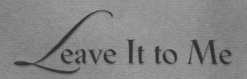 Leave It to Me

Mary Ellen once had a great burden in her life. She was so distraught that she was neither sleeping nor eating. It was jeopardizing her physical and emotional health, and she was on the verge of a nervous breakdown.

One day she read a magazine story about a woman named Connie who also faced major difficulties. Connie was able to bear up under the load of such troubles by taking her problems to God. "But we must not only *take* our problems there," Connie said. "We must *leave* our problems with the Lord."

There once was a man who vowed he would never ride in an airplane. But an emergency necessitated immediate travel to a distant city. So he purchased a ticket and made his first trip in an airplane. When his plane landed, his relatives asked him about his first flight. He responded, "Oh, it was all right, I guess. But I'll tell you one thing. I never let my *full weight* down on the seat." [20]

Even though the man could not relax in his seat, the airplane still carried him to his destination. The Lord wants you to cast your burdens on Him—and leave them there! He desires for you to give Him the full weight of your problems as well. Then you can go on with life in full confidence that He will take care of those things you have entrusted to Him.

Texas Limestone

Anita was determined to have a garden. She spent the entire hot, humid afternoon hacking away at the small plot of ground in the back of their central-Texas home. Farmers would call it "poor" soil—incapable of sustaining even the hardiest of vegetables. After about three inches, the soil gave way to limestone. Every time it seemed that she had found the last rock, sparks would fly from the blade as she again struck limestone. She grew weary and nearly gave up. It seemed that nothing would grow in this place. Yet she longed for a garden filled with ripe red tomatoes, green cucumbers, tall okra, and big ears of corn.

Slowly the soil began to turn more easily. Occasionally she would use the garden hose to dampen the dry earth as she removed the rocks. She then mixed in bags of new, rich topsoil and shaped the soil into smooth, parallel rows where she planted the vegetable seeds.

As with her garden, Anita also had to work hard to keep her heart right and free from the burdensome rocks of unforgiveness. She longed for healthy, merciful soil where seeds of God's love would yield a bumper crop of compassion and kindness. She knew that her daily choices in thought, word, and deed would determine whether her heart-garden was full of bitter rocks or joyful vegetation.

"Forgiveness is not an occasional act, it is a permanent attitude."
—Martin Luther King Jr.

How does your garden grow?

"OTHER FELL ON GOOD GROUND,

AND DID YIELD FRUIT."

MARK 4:8 KJV

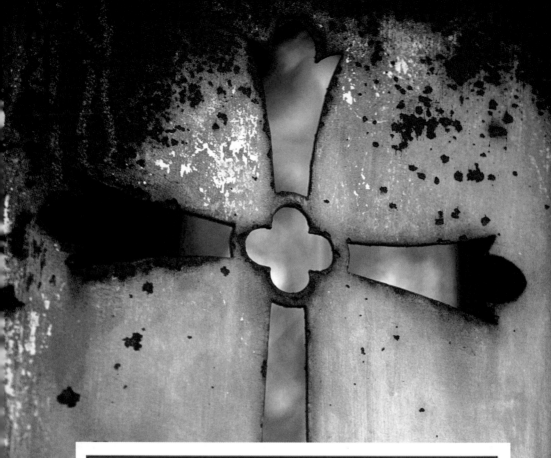

I KNOW THY WORKS, THAT THOU ART NEITHER COLD NOR HOT: I WOULD THOU WERT COLD OR HOT. SO THEN BECAUSE THOU ART LUKEWARM, AND NEITHER COLD NOR HOT, I WILL SPUE THEE OUT OF MY MOUTH.

REVELATION 3:15-16 KJV

No Room for Apathy

Indifferent. Uninvolved. Middle of the road. Riding the fence. Uncommitted. Undecided. That is what apathy means.

While we might think that apathy is a safe place in which to dwell, the Scriptures see it as a doomed existence. G.A. Studder-Kennedy's poem describes the Lord's sorrow over our apathy:

> When Jesus came to Golgotha,
> they hanged Him on a tree,
> They drove great nails through hand and feet
> and made a Calvary:
> They crowned Him with a crown of thorns,
> red were His wounds and deep,
> For those were crude and cruel days,
> and human flesh was cheap.
> When Jesus came in modern day,
> they simply passed Him by,
> They never hurt a hair of Him,
> they only let Him die:
> For men had grown more tender,
> and they would never give Him pain,
> They only just passed down the street
> and left Him in the rain.
> Still Jesus cried, "Forgive them,
> for they know not what they do;"
> And still it rained the winter rain
> that drenched Him through and through;
> The crowd went home and left the streets
> without a soul to see,
> And Jesus crouched against a wall
> and cried for Calvary.[21]

Choose passion over apathy today!

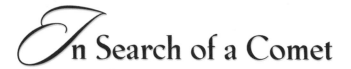

In Search of a Comet

"Get up, kids," Andrea called. "Let's go see the comet!"

The children groaned. "Are you crazy, Mom? It's three o'clock in the morning."

"This is a once-in-a-lifetime opportunity," she said. "It'll be fun!"

The family went in search of the famed Halley's comet. They parked in an open area, free of city lights and filled with nature's night sounds.

As they gazed up at the billions of stars sprinkled across the velvet black sky, sleepy eyes sparkled with wonder. The children pointed to the lights in the sky. "Is that it?" they would ask. Despite a diligent search, no one could identify the comet. Apparently, its appearance was not as spectacular as scientists had predicted. Still, the trip was worth it, and they excitedly continued to spot various constellations.

Andrea smiled and thought about how God's love is so much greater—so much more magnificent—than His creation. She could feel the blanket of His love wrapped around her family.

On the way home, they stopped at an all-night donut shop. After they had stuffed themselves, they sang funny songs in the car. Soon they were home, snugly tucked back into bed.

Some people would have called it a wild-goose chase, but Andrea called it an opportunity to share God's wondrous creation with her children. She went in search of Halley's comet. She found a more glorious sight: the joy of love.

AS HIGH AS THE HEAVENS

ARE ABOVE THE EARTH, SO GREAT IS HIS

LOVE FOR THOSE WHO FEAR HIM.

PSALM 103:11

THE GRASS WITHERS

AND THE FLOWERS FALL, BUT THE WORD

OF OUR GOD STANDS FOREVER.

ISAIAH 40:8

Changing Seasons

Marie enjoyed observing the changing seasons through her kitchen window. She watched a sparrow preparing her nest and then bringing food to her babies in the springtime. A hummingbird made regular stops all summer after it discovered the window feeder. Squirrels scampered around in the crisp fallen autumn leaves in search of nuts. And in winter, Marie spotted a deer in her yard.

Life is like the changing seasons. During the springtime of Marie's life, her days were filled with fun as she played with frogs and tadpoles. Her teen and young adult years—the summer of her life—were marked by enthusiasm as she tried to find herself in the fast lane of life. Today, Marie is beginning to sense the contentment of autumn. She sees security in the eyes of her husband and joy in the lives of her grown children. Soon winter will be upon her. Marie smiles as she reflects over the seasons of her life. Behind her are many wonderful memories, and ahead of her is the bright promise of eternal life.

There's nothing wrong with looking back at the previous seasons of our lives. But God has a purpose for allowing us to be in the season we're in right now. So enjoy where you're at on the way to where you're going!

LORD, THOU HAST BEEN OUR
DWELLING PLACE IN ALL GENERATIONS.

PSALM 90:1 KJV

Heart's Home

The home of Microsoft CEO, Bill Gates, has, not surprisingly, the latest in technological comforts and conveniences. A guest receives an electronic pin to clip to his or her clothing to identify who and where the guest is. This pin is programmed with individual interests and tastes. From room to room, the house adapts itself to those particular likes and dislikes. The temperature in each room automatically adjusts to the guest's preference. The music changes, and digital images appear on the walls of the rooms just before the guest enters and vanish after the guest leaves.

What happens if there is more than one person in the room? No problem! The computer selects programming that suits both tastes!

Technology can customize our homes to respond to our most immediate interests, tastes, and comfort levels. But there is something about the idea of "home" that goes well beyond physical surroundings. Home is a place where we can be ourselves. In that sense, there is a way in which no place on this planet will ever really be home for us.

In his work, *Thomas Wingfold, Curate,* George MacDonald wrote: "But there is that in us which is not at home in this world, which I believe holds secret relations with every star, or perhaps rather, with that in the heart of God whence issued every star. . . . To that in us, this world is so far strange and unnatural and unfitting, and we need a yet homelier home. Yea, no home at last will do, but the home of God's heart."

eferences

Endnotes

1 Kenneth W. Osbeck, *101 More Hymn Stories* (Grand Rapids, MI: Kregel Publications, 1985)

2 Robert Van de Weyer, ed., *Book of Prayers* (New York, NY: Harper Collins, 1993)

3 Ron Rand, "Won by One," Max Lucado, ed., *The Inspirational Study Bible* (Dallas, TX: Word, 1995)

4 Hazel Fellemen, ed., *The Best-Loved Poems of the American People* (New York, NY: Doubleday, 1936)

5 Toyohiko Kagawa and other Japanese poets, Lois J. Erickson, trans., *Songs from the Land of Dawn* (New York, NY: Friendship Press, 1949)

6 Jamie Buckingham, *The Last Word* (Plainfield: Logos, 1978)

7 Rueben P. Job and Norman Shawchuck, eds., *A Guide to Prayer for All God's People* (Nashville, TN: Upper Room Books, 1990)

8 John Barnett, *Carlsbad Caverns: Silent Chambers, Timeless Beauty* (Carlsbad, NM: Carlsbad Caverns-Guadalupe Mountains Association, 1981)

9 Tony Campolo, "Who Switched the Price Tags?" Max Lucado. ed., *The Inspirational Study Bible* (Dallas, TX: Word, 1995)

10 James W. Hewett, ed., *Illustrations Unlimited* (Wheaton, IL: Tyndale, 1988)

11 Louis Haskins, "Introduction," Mrs. Charles Cowan, ed., *Traveling Toward Sunrise* (Grand Rapids, MI: Zondervan, [no pub date])

12 Tyron Edwards, *The New Dictionary of Thoughts* (New York, NY: Standard, 1963)

13 Patricia Gentry, *Teatime Collections* (San Ramon, CA: Chevron Chemical, 1988)

14 Billy Graham, *Unto the Hills: A Devotional Treasury* (Waco, TX: Word, 1986)

15 *Good Housekeeping,* February 1996.

16 Billy Graham, *Unto the Hills: A Devotional Treasury* (Waco, TX: Word, 1986)

17 Glenn Park, *The Man Who Talks with the Flowers* (St. Paul, MN: Macalester, 1939)

Additional copies of this book and other titles
in the Quiet Moments with God Devotional series
are available from your local bookstore.

Clothbound devotionals:

Breakfast with God   Coffee Break with God
Sunset with God   Tea Time with God
Daybreak with God   Through the Night with God
In the Garden with God   In the Kitchen with God
Christmas with God

Portable gift editions:

Breakfast with God   Coffee Break with God
Sunset with God   Tea Time with God

If you have enjoyed this book, or if it has impacted your life,
we would like to hear from you. Please contact us at:

Honor Books
Department E
P.O. Box 55388
Tulsa, Oklahoma 74155

Or, by e-mail at info@honorbooks.com

Tulsa, Oklahoma